AF479828

Mr.4000 takes the City of Dreams

By Dante Moore

Pictures By Megan Rizzo

Copyright (c) 2023 by Dante Moore

ISBN: 979-8-218-29328-4

All rights reserved. No part of this book may be reproduced or transmitted in any form or by any means, electronic or mechanical, including photocopying, recording, or by any information storage and retrieval system, without permission in writing from the copyright owner.

This book was printed in the United States of America.

This book is dedicated to my family.
I appreciate everyone's sacrifices, it has
made us who we are, today!

Dante was five years old and had just moved from East Cleveland, Ohio to Detroit, MI. He loved playing sports, more than anything, especially basketball and soccer. So, after school, Dante would grab his basketball and soccer ball, and take turns playing each one, dribbling and kicking with all his might.

"Dante! It's time to come in for the night!" Mr. Moore would often have to call for him, signaling for Dante to come into the house.

There are so many sports to play.
How will I chose?

Dante's dad was sitting at the dinner table, when Dante walked in. They met eyes, and Mr. Moore smiled warmly before saying, "Guess what, champ? You're joining my football team!" Dante looked unsure, his little face scrunched up, and he said, "But Dad, I'm not sure I want to..." Dad assured him, "Trust me, you'll have a blast!"

Dante started to work out with his dad. He loved sports, but he did not know if he would be good at playing with a team.

As Dante began to play with his team and faced off against other teams, he saw his hard work paying off. One sunny day, he made a spectacular catch during practice, the ball sticking right in his small hands.

It was common for people to tell him, "Wow, you can catch and throw really well!"

Kids on the team clapped and shouted, "Dante, you're amazing!" Dante couldn't help but grin, "Maybe I do like football!"

As Dante's interest and talent grew in football, many people came around, having a direct impact on his confidence. One person was Uncle Chop, who had always been his biggest supporter.

One day, Dante's uncle, Uncle Chop, puffed out his chest proudly and told him, "You're going to be a star, Mr. 4000!"

Dante's eyes sparkled with curiosity, "Mr. 4000? That sounds cool!" Uncle Chop gave him a warm hug, "You've got a gift, Dante. Use it wisely."

Dante took his uncle's advice to heart. He worked hard at being a great player, practicing catches in the backyard until the sun dipped below the horizon. But he also worked at being a great student, studying late into the night. His dream was to be the best student-athlete he could be.

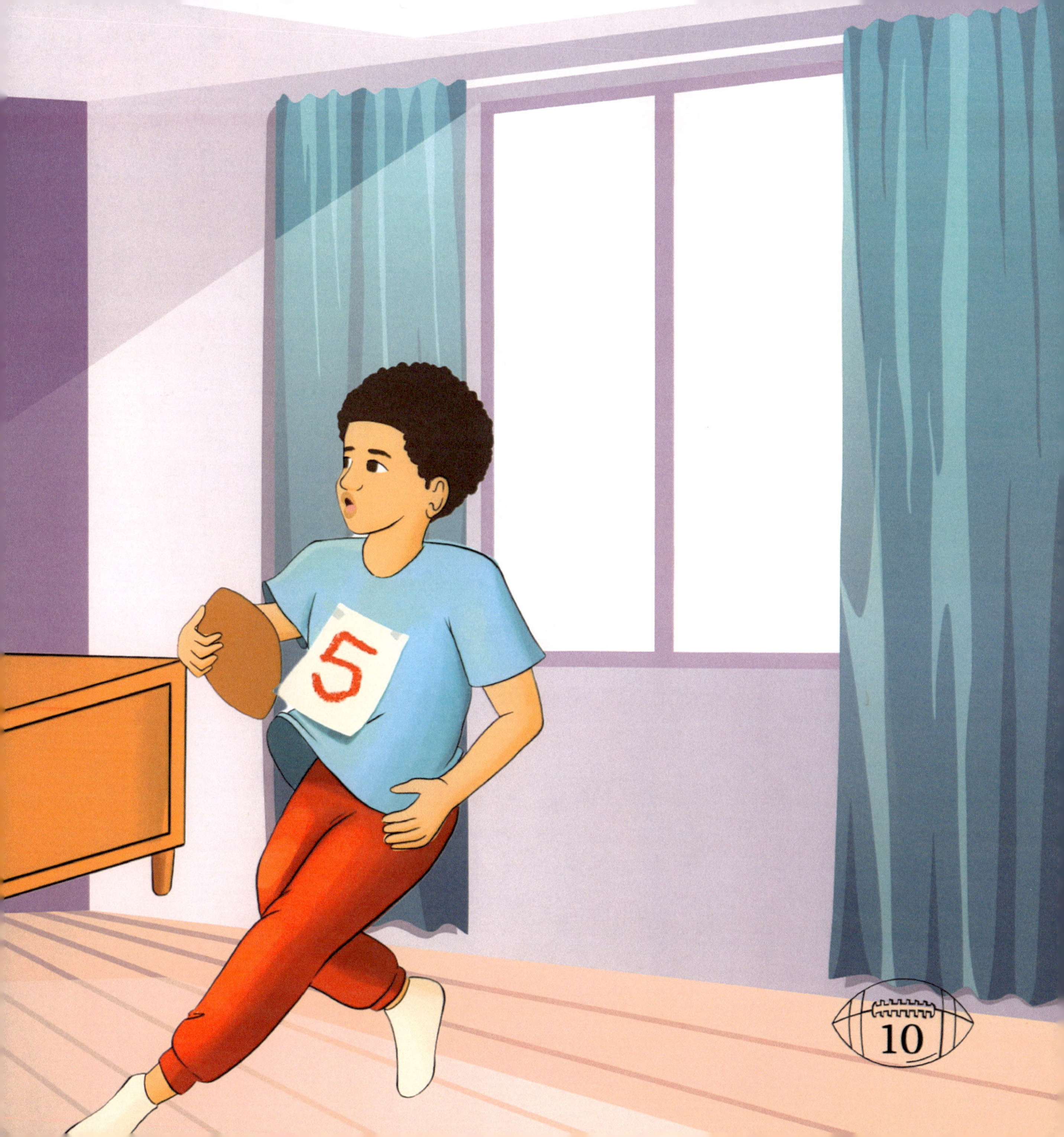
5

Along Dante's journey, he continued to cross paths with coaches that had a big impact on him. One of Dante's favorite coaches, Coach KG, was his little league coach. Coach saw the leader in Dante, and he'd always tell him, "Dante, you're a secret weapon!"

Dante knew that he had to be a team player if he wanted to be great. He encouraged his teammates, shouting words of support from the sidelines and always making sure to give them credit. He believed that he couldn't be great without them.

After little league, Dante went on to high school., where he played for a winning team. He was a star quarterback amongst his team, and around the country. Colleges all over the US, wanted Dante to play football at their school, and he was challenged with deciding which school would be the best fit, for him.

In the past, his father would help him choose a team, but now, Dante had to use all the lessons from his journey to help him make a decision.

I want a great coach and a great team. I'd love it to be warm, year round.

Dante faced a tough decision, one that would shape his future. He remembered the lessons he had learned along his incredible journey – the hard work, the teamwork, and the unwavering support of his family and mentors.

In the end, Dante chose a school where he felt not only could he be a great football player but also a great student and leader. As he stepped onto the college campus, he knew that his adventure was just beginning. With every touchdown pass and every A on his report card, Dante continued to make his family, his mentors, and his community proud.

Just like Dante, you have the power to turn your dreams into reality. Believe in yourself, work hard, and never give up. With determination, teamwork, and the support of those who believe in you, there's no limit to what you can achieve.

Your journey is just beginning, and every step you take brings you closer to your own shining star. Keep chasing your dreams and making a difference in the world. You are capable of greatness, and your story is waiting to be written."

Photo provided by Dante Moore.

FROM JOURNEY, TO DREAM

It's your turn to talk about your dream. Tell me who or what you want to do when you graduate high school? You also have to tell me 3 things you can do to help you achieve your dream!

www.ingramcontent.com/pod-product-compliance
Lightning Source LLC
Chambersburg PA
CBRC091646100726
47973CB00020B/245

9798218293284